COUNTING BACKWARDS

COUNTING BACKWARDS 10-1

Missing Numbers from 10-1

Missing Numbers from 10-1

Missing Numbers from 10-1

Missing Numbers from 10-1

Missing Numbers from 10-1

Missing Numbers from 10-1

Missing Numbers from 10-1

Missing Numbers from 10-1

Missing Numbers from 10-1

COUNTING BACKWARDS
20-1

Missing Numbers from 20-1

Missing Numbers from 20-1

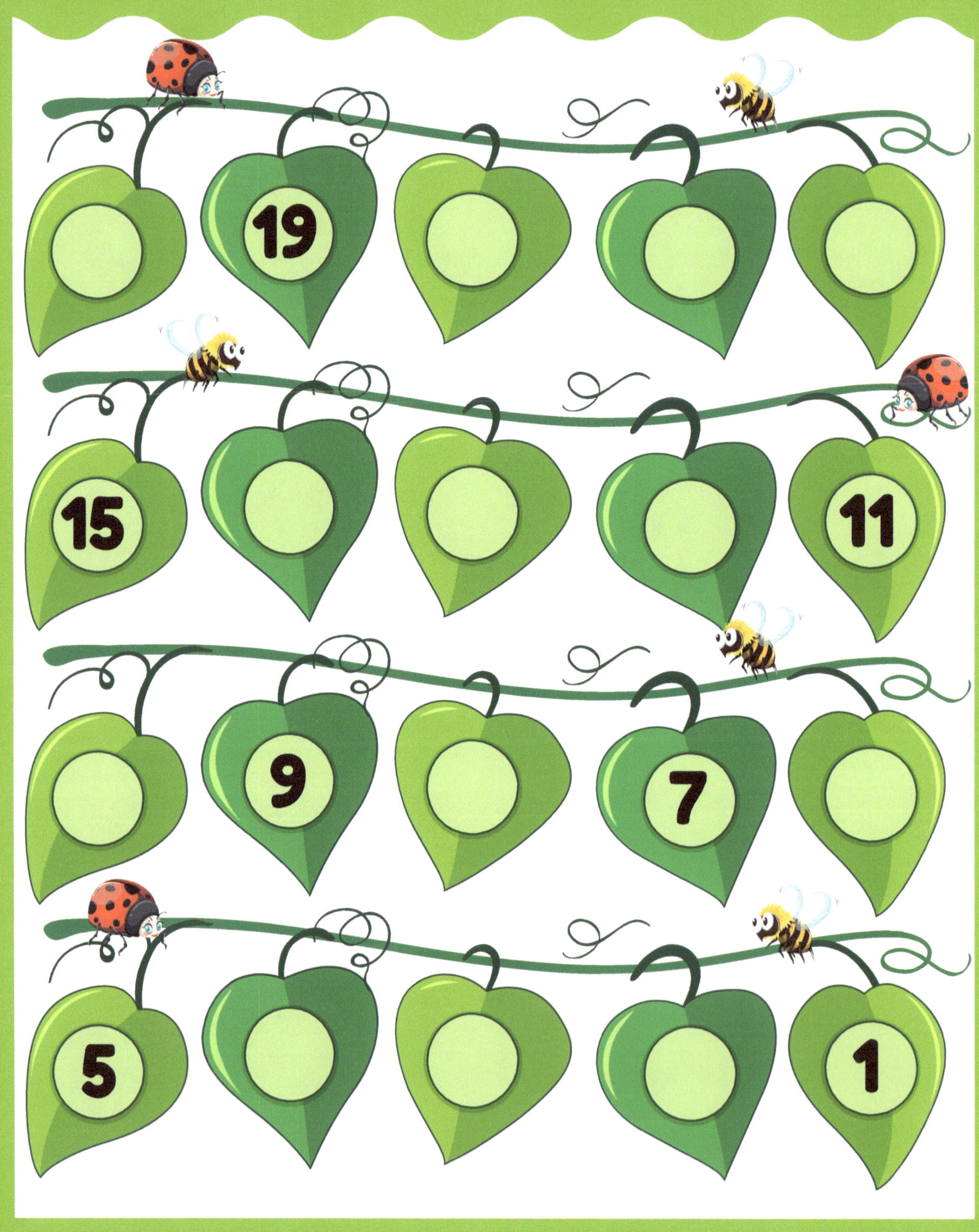

Missing Numbers from 20-1

Missing Numbers from 20-1

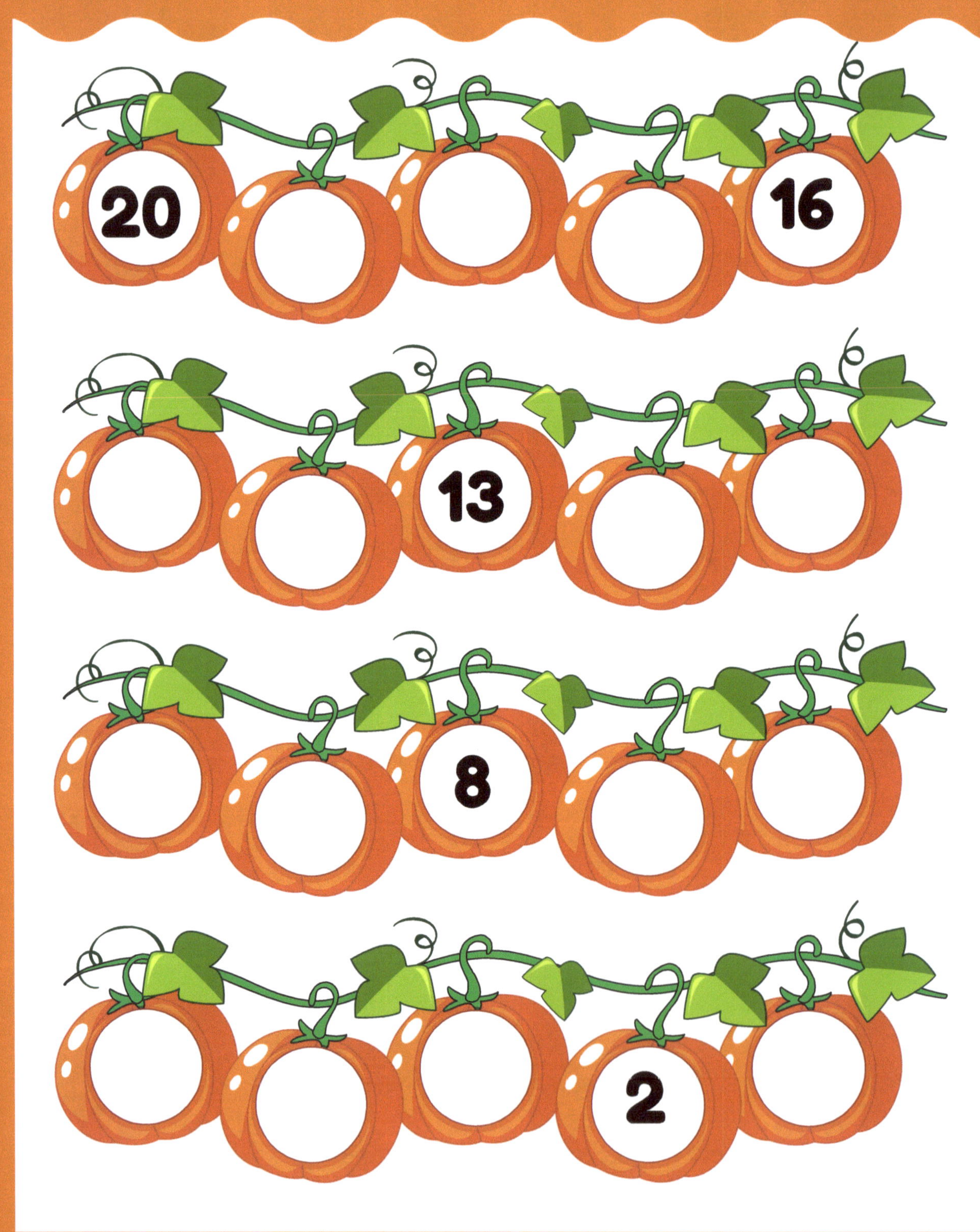

Missing Numbers from 20-1

Missing Numbers from 20-1

Missing Numbers from 20-1

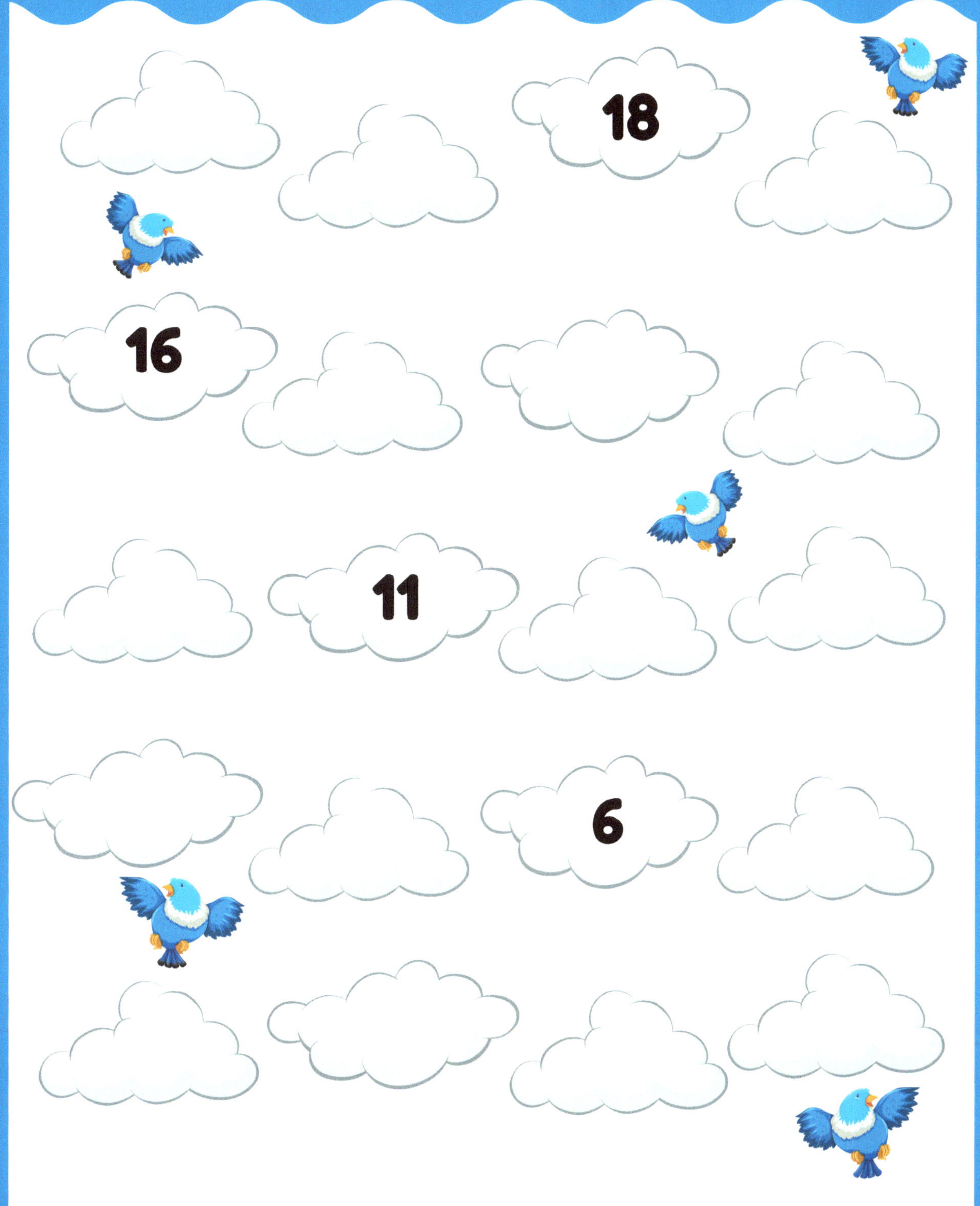

Missing Numbers from 20-1

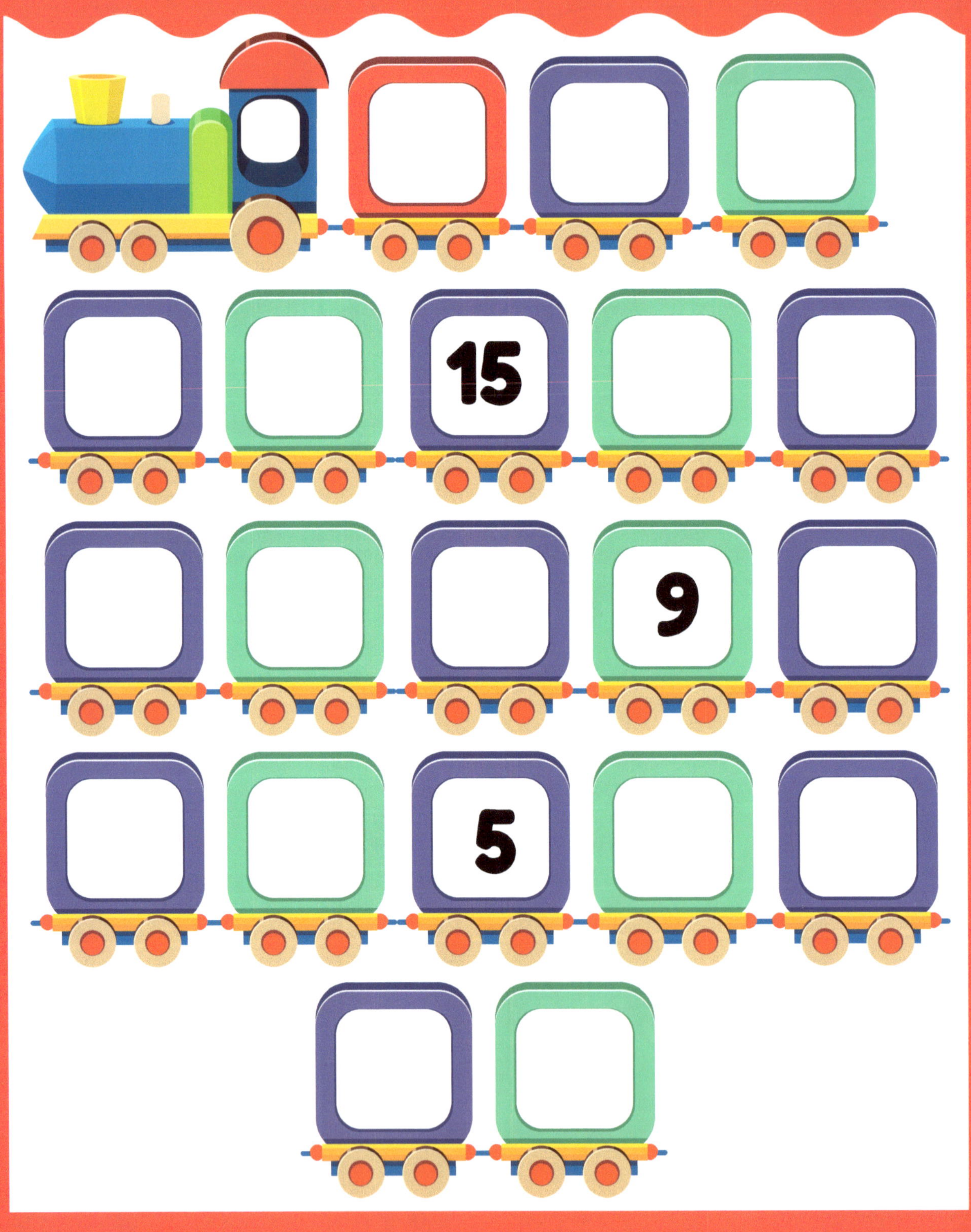

Missing Numbers from 20-1

COUNTING BACKWARDS 100-1

Missing Numbers from 100-1

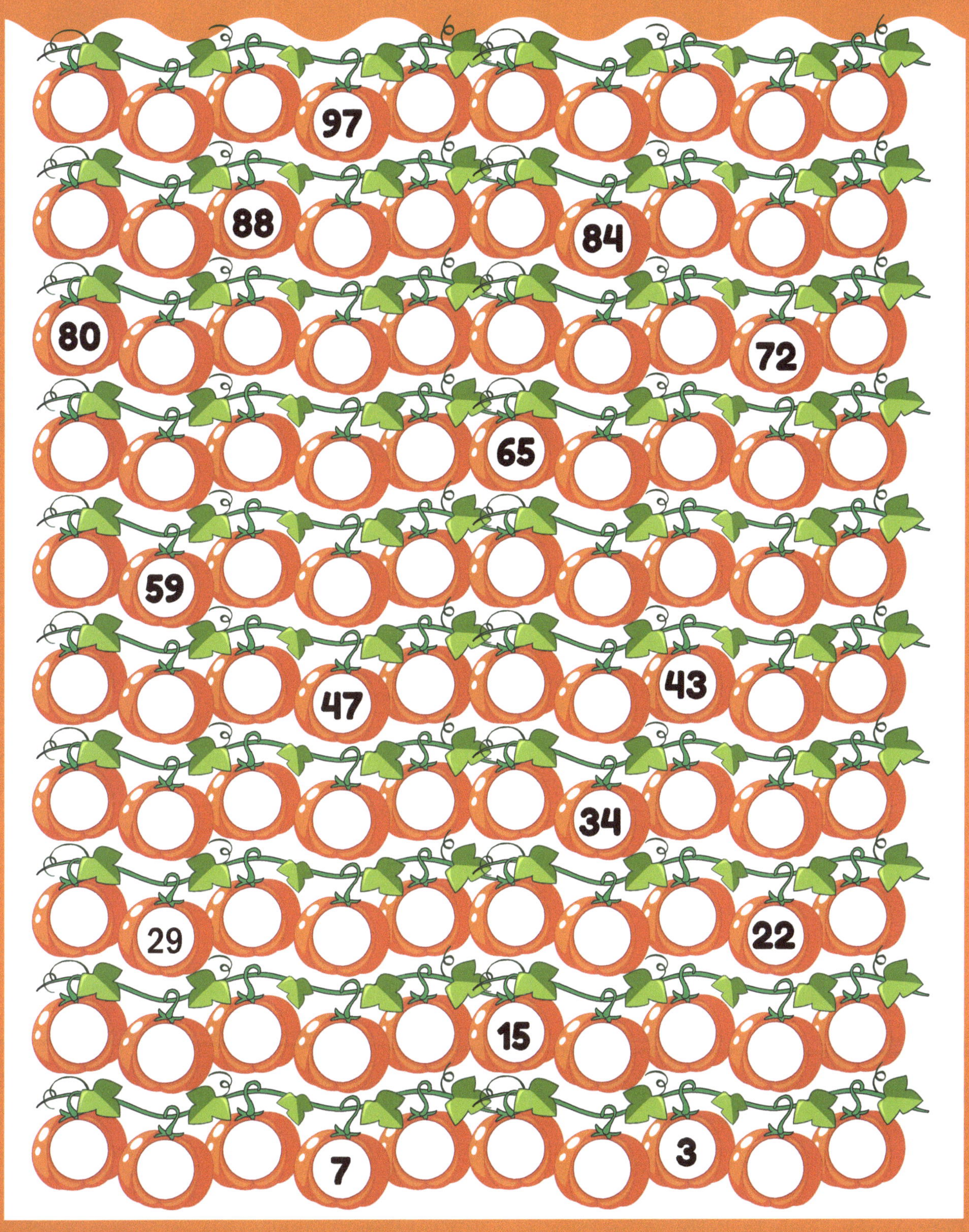

Missing Numbers from 100-1

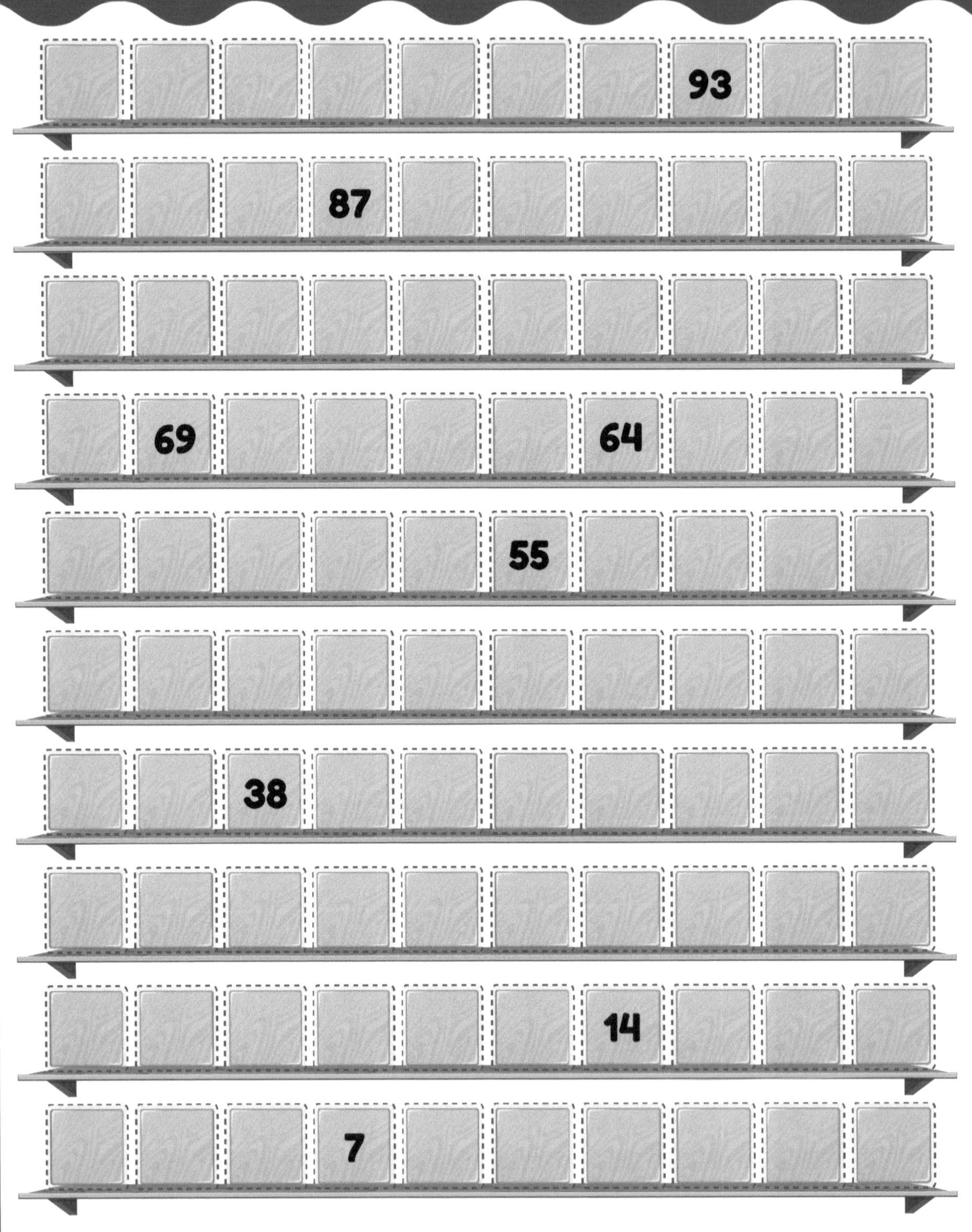

Missing Numbers from 100-1